W9-BZB-651

USING COMPUTER SCIENCE IN MILITARY »SERVICE«

XINA M. UHL

Sparrows Point High School
Baltimore County Public Schools

Rosen
YA™

New York

For Kyle

Published in 2019 by The Rosen Publishing Group, Inc.
29 East 21st Street, New York, NY 10010

Library of Congress Cataloging-in-Publication Data

Names: Ulh, Xina M., author.
Title: Using computer science in military service / Xina M. Uhl.
Description: New York : Rosen YA, 2019 | Series: Coding your passion | Includes bibliographical references and index. | Audience: Grades 7–12.
Identifiers: LCCN 2018011833| ISBN 9781508183990 (library bound) | ISBN 9781508184010 (pbk.)
Subjects: LCSH: United States—Armed Forces—Vocational guidance—Juvenile literature. | Computer science—Vocational guidance—Juvenile literature.
Classification: LCC UB147 .U44 2019 | DDC 355.0023/73—dc23
LC record available at https://lccn.loc.gov/2018011833

Manufactured in the United States of America

CONTENTS

INTRODUCTION

Just as in everyday life, business, and education, computers have made a tremendous impact on the military. Over the last thirty years, this role has increased exponentially. Computers are used for gathering and analyzing intelligence, identifying and organizing data, coordinating location information, operating smart weapons, exchanging communications, and countless administrative and logistical tasks.

Historically, military operations have bogged down due to slow communications, inaccurate intelligence, and problems with the supply chain. Computers improve each of these areas to the degree that casualties, both in the military and the civilian population, have dropped dramatically. According to the US Department of Veterans Affairs, deaths in the American Civil War (1861–1865) equaled 15 percent of those who served. In the Gulf Wars in the early 1990s, that rate had fallen to .0006 percent. Advances in medicine contributed to that decrease, certainly. So did lessons learned from previous conflicts and that were applied during training. But technology accounted for much of that decrease as well. The ability to utilize advanced technology in air strikes, positioning of ground troops, communications, and strategy has forever changed the face of warfare.

Two members of the US Navy's Unmanned Aerial Vehicle Squadron troubleshoot an RQ21A drone aboard the USS *Mesa Verde*. The drone will be used in an upcoming deployment.

The primary role of the US military is defending the nation. As such, computers will continue to be integrated into weapons, such as guided missiles, drones, and other aircraft. Protective devices and armor will utilize sensors and computer technology. Medical advances continue to increase survival rate as well. Computers play a vital role in day-to-day functions, such as payroll distribution. However, the dawn of the twenty-first century has brought with it threats that have not previously been faced, such as cyberwarfare.

At the time of this writing, more than one million active-duty military personnel are enlisted into the different branches of the American military. This is supplemented by the more than 230,000 active-duty officers. Enlisted personnel make up about 82 percent of the armed forces. Their function is to carry out military operations. The remaining 18 percent are officers who lead troops, manage enlisted personnel, and coordinate operations. About 8 percent of officers are warrant officers, who are technical and tactical experts in a specific area. Army aviators, for example, make up one group of warrant officers.

Computer science careers in the military are available throughout all branches in all occupational groups to one degree or another. Civilian contractors may also be employed for specialized support roles. The Bureau of Labor Statistics' *Occupational Outlook Handbook* predicts that qualified individuals have a very good job outlook through 2026. All services need to fill positions at all levels and offer opportunities for advancement throughout the length of service.

This volume examines computer science careers, outlooks, preparation, and technological advances in progress and on the horizon. Recruitment in the armed forces remains strong. A career in computer coding is unlike many because you can begin preparing for it right now. Coders have many opportunities online and in local and educational venues to teach themselves coding skills and to prepare themselves for other aspects of military service. Clubs, computer camps, and classes at your school are good places to start if you don't want to explore the internet on your own for tutorials. Joining your school's Reserve Officers' Training Corps (ROTC) or Junior Reserve Officers' Training Corps (JROTC) is worth looking into because it can provide preparation for military life.

THE RISE OF MILITARY TECHNOLOGY

The modern computer era can be traced to the Cold War between the United States and the Soviet Union, during the second half of the twentieth century. The war was described as "cold" because it largely didn't involve combat. It was a struggle of ideals. On one side, democracy and the United States, and on the other, communism and the Soviet Union—two forms of government at odds with one another. The superpowers tried to prove the superiority of their governments through technological advances, among other efforts.

In the late 1950s, the Soviet Union pulled ahead technologically. It launched the first man-made object into Earth's orbit—*Sputnik*. The United States decided not to let the Soviets take first place in space, and so the space race was on.

In 1958, the government created the National Aeronautics and Space Administration (NASA) to explore space. A number of developments occurred

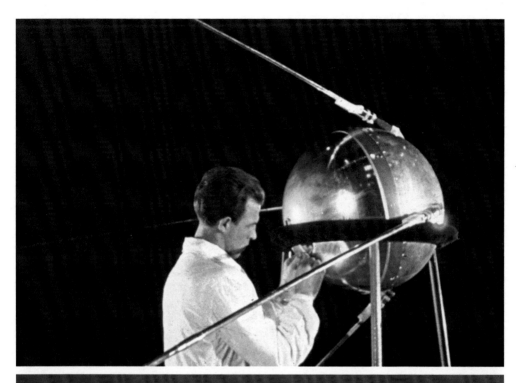

A Soviet technician works on *Sputnik 1* in 1957. The world's first artificial satellite, *Sputnik 1* weighed 183.9 pounds (83.6 kilograms) and orbited the Earth in about ninety-eight minutes.

in both superpowers as the race heated up over the years, designing, testing, and launching new space vehicles, such as the Soviets' *Vostok 1* and the US Apollo program. The United States declared victory in the race when, on July 16, 1969, American astronaut Neil Armstrong became the first person to walk on the moon.

NASA engineers would not have succeeded if they hadn't made significant advances in computer technology. These advances carried over into the private sector. They led to the invention of the internet, smartphones, and digital technology. Laptop computers, the joystick, virtual reality, 3D graphics, satellite navigation, artificial limbs, satellite TV, smoke detectors, and much more came from NASA's advances.

THE EVOLUTION OF WARFARE TECHNOLOGY

From the beginning of time, humans have waged war on one another. Stones that were chipped in order to form a blade have been used as tools and weapons for hundreds of thousands of years. The first arrowheads appeared more than sixty thousand years ago. Following them were other weapons, such as the spear, javelin, and sling. However, the earliest weapon designed for war was the mace, a blunt weapon that appeared in the fifth and fourth millennia BCE. Unlike later maces made from metals that sported pointed ends, these early maces were rocks attached to a handle, used to smash an opponent's bones. Later maces were made from copper, bronze, or iron. The use of metals increased their deadly power.

Improvements to axes, spears, javelins, and slings followed from around 1000 BCE to AD 400. The short sword was a favorite weapon of Roman troops. Defensive armor such as helmets, shields, and body armor also appeared in this era. Other than hand weapons and those powered by human might, such as the bow and arrow, this period saw the invention of mechanical artillery such as a type of catapult, large crossbows, and siege towers used to approach and breach the walls of enemy forts or cities.

LIVING WEAPONS

War elephants were used in antiquity in India, Persia, and in civilizations located around the Mediterranean Sea. Four-wheeled carts drawn by donkeys were used for battle in Sumer around 2500 BCE. Chariots developed after this, appearing in Iran around 1600 BCE. These vehicles generally had two wheels and were pulled by two to three horses.

The age of cavalry, or the use of horses for war, lasted from CE 400–1350. By the fourth century CE, the Chinese developed stirrups from iron and bronze. They enabled horseback riders to control their mounts more efficiently. Nomad tribespeople, such as the Huns and Avars, employed archers who shot from horseback by around the sixth and seventh centuries, though stirrups did not come into wide use in Europe until the eighth century. The Turks and Mongols were also skilled archers from horseback.

Over the next few centuries war horses, specially bred and trained for combat, were used in medieval Europe. Armored knights would ride such animals and make use of long, heavy lances to disarm and unhorse opponents. Fulfilling the needs of such war horses involved a significant amount of time and money. Not only do the animals require substantial food, but they need training and vet care as well.

GUNPOWDER

The next major advance in the technology of warfare was the discovery and development of weapons using gunpowder. The Chinese developed black powder in the ninth century and used it for fireworks and crude cannons, but little else. Mongols in the thirteenth century likely brought black powder to Europe, where it evolved over several centuries into potent weapons that include muzzleloaders, cannons, matchlocks, wheel locks, and flintlocks.

The American Civil War marked a turning point in warfare due to the use of rifles, which increased the range and effectiveness of bullets from that of a musket—about 250 yards (229 meters)—to around 1,000 yards (914 m).

MODERN TIMES

Technological advances in warfare only increased after the Civil War. World War I (1914–1918) brought into use the tank, chemical warfare, tracer bullets for nighttime battles, aircraft, and aircraft carriers. Underwater bombs called depth charges were used to devastating effect by German submarines called U-boats.

World War II (1939–1945) saw the improvement and widening use of earlier technologies, such as the tank, aircraft, and explosives. As a result, they played a greater role in warfare. Tanks became stronger and tougher, allowing Adolf Hitler to take over much of Europe. Fighter jets engaged in air-to-air combat and

The US military forces made use of 183 aircraft during World War II (1939–1945). Fighter jets often engaged in aerial combat with enemy planes.

dropped bombs on enemy targets. Aircraft carriers grew bigger and allowed militaries to launch air attacks from oceans the world over. Radar used radio waves to locate enemy aircraft. Bombs became more accurate. The atomic bomb was developed in secret. Its detonation over the Japanese cities Hiroshima and Nagasaki, and the destruction and death it caused, convinced Japan's leadership to end the war in the Pacific.

THE MANHATTAN PROJECT

When scientists discovered that German physicists had succeeded in splitting uranium atoms in 1939, it caused alarm. Albert Einstein wrote to President Franklin D. Roosevelt to express his concern that Germany would develop bombs capable of unheard-of destruction.

In order to keep Germany from developing a bomb before the United States, Roosevelt authorized a secret effort in 1941 to research atomic energy called the Manhattan Project. Many scientists who had fled Germany helped American scientists and others develop the atomic bomb. By the project's end, about two hundred thousand people had worked on it and $2 billion had been spent. But it had succeeded in creating an atomic bomb.

The bomb was first tested in the New Mexico desert in July 1945. The explosion was 18,000 times greater than that of a ton of TNT. It was so great that they feared the use of it. In his diary in 1945, President Harry Truman wrote, "We have discovered the most terrible bomb in the history of the world."

English inventor Charles Babbage came up with the design for a computer in the 1830s, but it was not until the 1940s that the first electronic computers came into existence. After World War II, engineer Claude Shannon helped to develop binary programming. The most basic unit of information within a computer is called a bit, or binary digit. Binary code consists of 1s and 0s. When grouped together, these bits are known as bytes. They can be arranged in patterns to instruct computers to perform specific actions.

Early computers were gigantic. Instructions for a computer's operation, or code, was input into room-sized computing machines via hole-punched cards or by inserting and unplugging a series of wires into and out of a circuit board. This code was slow and unwieldy. The development of programming languages speeded up the process by creating common computer instructions using words or phrases. Developing programs became easier, yet they did not always work perfectly. They often needed to be fixed, or debugged.

Most early systems had to use specially designed hardware and software. Line commands instructed the computer in ways similar to coding and algorithms. Different computer languages were developed to create programs specific to government and businesses.

In 1969, the US Department of Defense developed ARPANET, the Advanced Research Projects Agency Network, an early computer network, as a means of linking universities and research groups working on defense together. It was the inspiration for the development of the internet in the 1980s.

CHAPTER TWO

MILITARY COMPUTING

The armed forces is a well-functioning machine, one that has been tested by time and through many battles. The four major branches—the US Army, Air Force, Navy, and Marines—and the Coast Guard have many similarities. They also have important differences. What is uniform across them is the need for computers in applications from communications to medicine to defense and administration. The way the military uses computers is different from civilian life and private industry. Let's take a bird's-eye view of the military's organization to start.

TAKING THE RIGHT PATH

You're probably familiar with standardized tests, such as the SAT or ACT, which are designed to predict your success in college. The military has its own test,

US Army Private First Class (PFC) Brian Juno makes use of computer software at Fort Riley, Kansas, to practice the duties of a convoy gunner.

the Armed Services Vocational Aptitude Battery, or ASVAB. This multiple-choice test is different from other standardized tests because it does not grade your fitness for college. Instead, it tests your general knowledge and fitness for military service. It covers ten areas: general science, arithmetic reasoning, word knowledge, paragraph comprehension, numerical operations, coding speed, auto and shop information, mathematics knowledge, mechanical comprehension, and electronics information.

The test's ten areas will take approximately three hours to complete, and the test usually is administered by your school, though it may be taken at Military Entrance Test (MET) sites. Each test is valid for two years. The ASVAB's scores help administrators match your skills and education level to the best possible military occupational specialty (MOS). Your assigned MOS will dictate the additional training you will need if you are accepted into service.

The military branches convert the ASVAB test scores into composite score areas. For the army, the most important ASVAB score is the Armed Forces Qualification Test, or AFQT. It covers paragraph comprehension, word knowledge, mathematics knowledge, and arithmetic reasoning. Examples of other composite score areas that are particularly related to coding are electronics (EL), general maintenance (GM), and skilled technical (ST). Though they differ in content, each of these relies heavily on science, math, and arithmetic reasoning.

Your ASVAB scores will help you assess whether the career path you had in mind is a good fit for what the military has to offer. If you haven't already decided on a general path to take, your ASVAB scores will provide solid direction. If you earn a college degree before joining the military, you are eligible to become an officer. If you don't, you may join as an enlisted person. Warrant officers may be drawn from enlisted ranks and bridge the gap between officers and the enlisted. They usually serve in highly specialized technical positions. Each path has advantages and disadvantages, but many people choose to enlist in the military to enjoy benefits such as travel and money to pay for college or trade schools.

CRYPTOLOGY

The army's cryptologic cyberspace intelligence collector/analyst position is an example of a military job in the field of cryptology, or the study, writing, and solving of codes, that involves the use of advanced computing. The person in this position uses computers to analyze codes to identify military targets. Job duties include collecting and processing data and reporting to superiors with information detected. Training involves twenty-six weeks of advanced individual and on-the-job instruction. This position qualifies for the PaYS Program and partners with companies such as Lockheed Martin for interviews after discharge.

The navy has a number of positions in cryptology under the oversight of Cryptologic Warfare Officers. Technician jobs include individuals who interpret languages, maintain systems, serve as radar signal experts and signal interceptors, and network experts.

The air force employs cryptology analysts and technicians in various capacities.

THE FIVE BRANCHES

Each branch of service has its own unique roles and focuses. The army is the oldest and largest branch. It is considered the military's ground force and is mainly responsible for protecting US security and that of its interests. It consists of full-time enlistment, known as active duty, and part-time enlistment that can become active duty during times of need. The Army Reserve and Army National Guard are part-time services.

The navy is the defender of the right to travel and trade on the world's seas. It also supports the air force's missions by providing aircraft runways and

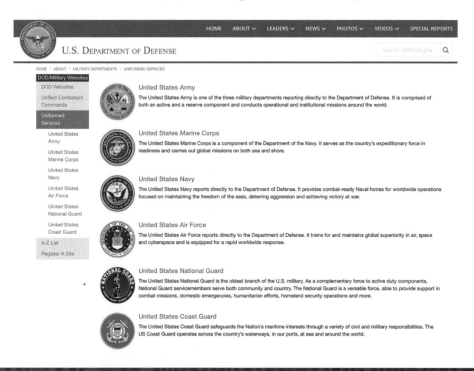

The US Department of Defense's website (https://www.defense.gov) details the nation's military branches, including the United States National Guard, which assists the active duty forces.

transportation of vehicles. The Navy Reserve is the part-time component.

The Marine Corps is the second-smallest branch. Originally under the authority of the navy, it has been a separate branch specializing in ground combat since 1798. Its part-time component is the Marine Corps Reserve.

The air force was established in 1947 for the purpose of protecting US security in the air and space. It contains two-part time options: Air Force Reserve and Air National Guard.

Finally, the Coast Guard is the smallest branch of the military, tasked with protecting US waterways.

US Navy Quartermaster 3rd Class Sharon Stone works on a computer on the bridge of the USS *Ashland* as it patrols the Indo-Asia-Pacific region.

During wartime, it is deployed with the navy. Since 2002, it has fallen under the Department of Homeland Security, though it is administered by the Department of the Navy during situations of need. The part-time service is the Coast Guard Reserve.

THE MILITARY'S COMPUTER STRATEGY

Military leadership has identified five strategic initiatives that utilize computer technology. These areas direct the military's efforts for future developments. If you are interested in cutting-edge technology, pay attention to these priorities.

1. Creating machines that are able to adapt to changing circumstances and learn from experience.
2. Human-machine collaborations that help humans to process large amounts of information.
3. Wearable technology and lightweight communications gear for battlefield use.
4. Human-machine combat teams.
5. Weapons that communicate with each other to update and identify new targets.

Each of these priorities means the modern military puts a premium on the development of artificial intelligence, robotics, cyberweapons, and advanced prostheses.

Rank and pay rate structure are the same across all branches. For computer careers, the navy and air force have the biggest focus on technology, though every branch includes computers in many different capacities.

DIFFERENCES FROM CIVILIAN WORK

Computer coding skills are highly valued in the military and in civilian careers. But what can you expect when you join the military? Civilian workers are rarely required to have the level of personal responsibility necessary as members of the military. After all, active combat means you may risk your life or be responsible for the lives of others. In the absence of that, daily routines may be similar. In the civilian world, you need to worry about your education, paying for your own living arrangements, food, clothing, and medical care. All that is taken care of in the military.

Basic pay in the military comes with tax advantages not available to civilians. Civilian pay is usually higher, however. Health care, housing, and insurance are provided to members of the military. You may be able to live off base and receive a tax-free Basic Allowance for Housing. Civilians are responsible for their own arrangements in these areas, but are also likely to have more choices available.

The GI Bill provides undergraduate and graduate educational benefits unavailable to civilians. Travel is usually necessary depending on where you are stationed as a military member and is covered by the government. In civilian life, travel not required by your workplace must be paid for by you. In the military, you are guaranteed thirty days of vacation a year. While this varies in the civilian world, most employers offer some paid vacation days per year.

Military work hours may involve weekend work, but otherwise usually involves weekdays. You are on call every day, twenty-four hours a day. Civilians usually work forty hours a week, though this can vary.

Finally, some members of the military can retire after fifteen years of active-duty service, though most must put in twenty years. This varies greatly for civilians. Most employers require thirty-five or more years before retirement is a possibility.

CHAPTER THREE

THE TECHNOLOGY OF WEAPONRY

The military's most fundamental duty is to protect the nation and its interests from harm. When diplomacy has failed, when it is necessary to respond to attacks that have already occurred or when violence is inevitable, military force may need to be employed. From humanity's earliest days, humans have fought one another with fists, clubs, spears, arrows, swords, muskets, rifles, and more. Over time, technology allowed weaponry to become more advanced.

Projectile weapons have an obvious advantage: distance. It is safer for warriors and armies to inflict damage on enemy territory while preserving their own health and safety. The Chinese first developed gunpowder in the eleventh century. By placing it in paper packets and attaching a fuse, the soldier could place the packet on an arrow and fire it toward the enemy, where it would explode. Advances followed from this, such as cannons, rockets, and exploding shells. Modern bombs evolved from the discovery of gunpowder. They carry an explosive charge to create destruction and are often dropped from aircraft.

The science of bomb-making has become ever more sophisticated, allowing for the creation of devices that blast, fragment, pierce armor, and release fire. More destructive explosives, such as ammonium nitrate, are used, and bombs are dropped from airplanes to the ground. These are conventional weapons, and accuracy has always been difficult to achieve when, for instance, World War II bombardiers released bombs from moving aircraft to targets on the ground.

CODING BOMBS AND MISSILES

Smart bombs fitted with wings, adjustable fins, and small lasers or camera guidance systems increase accuracy. The use of lasers involves an aircraft beaming a laser at a target. The bomb's sensors pick up the beam and follow it to the target. Camera guidance units transmit images of targets to an aircraft crew or a computer, and guide it to the target. Such advanced technology requires computer experts to design, build, and maintain it.

One example of advanced technology is the Tomahawk cruise missile. One missile can fly 550 miles (885 km) per hour 100 feet (30 m) above ground, allowing it to avoid radar detection by the

A Royal Danish Air Force GBU-58 smart bomb appears under the wing of an F-16A during NATO's Operation Unified Protector.

enemy. It makes use of GPS communications for long-range, fixed-target location. The first Tomahawk missile was used during Operation Desert Storm in 1991. A more recent upgrade, Block IV Tomahawk missiles, have a range of 1,000 miles (1,600 km). Upgrades are being produced on a regular basis and incorporate advanced computer systems. These systems require expert coders.

SMART BULLETS

Sandia National Laboratories in Albuquerque, New Mexico, and Livermore, California, are developing self-guided bullets that can hit targets more than 1 mile (1.6 km) away. These 4-inch- (10.16 cm) long smart bullets can move left, right, up, and down—and even change direction in midflight—in order to strike targets.

The bullet technology was developed by engineers Red Jones and Brian Kast, who are also hunters. They believe that a private company partnership would allow them to develop the bullets quickly and inexpensively. Those interested in such ammunition may include law enforcement, the military, and recreational shooters. As far as the military is concerned, though, there's one big problem to overcome: the bullets move 600 feet (200 meters) per second slower than regular rifle bullets. However, this is likely to be solved over time.

ADVANCED WARPLANE AND WEAPONS SYSTEMS

Computer simulations are used to train military recruits in developments in missiles, bombs, and other weapons systems. Since such activities occur in a

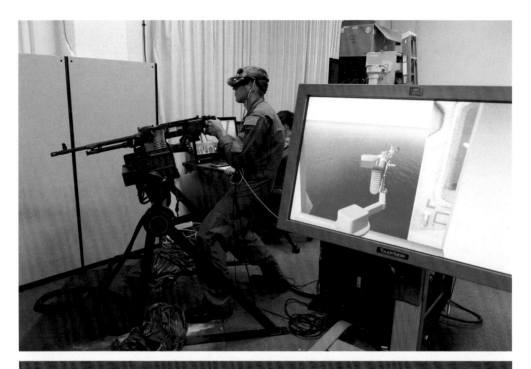

Naval Aircrewman 3rd Class David Finley demonstrates a training simulator on Ford Island, Hawaii. The simulator makes use of gaming technology to sharpen combatants' skills.

simulated environment rather than in real-world tests on land or at sea, these simulations are both less costly and less dangerous to equipment and personnel.

Current weapons systems rely heavily on computers to function, such as the Common Remotely Operated Weapon Station, or CROWS. This device is mounted atop small armored vehicles. Soldiers inside the vehicle can access 360-degree video while inside, as well as deploy machine guns, grenade launchers, or other weapons. It can operate during the day or night and includes a thermal camera to sense heat.

Though computer technology in weaponry has many advantages, it can cause problems. Described by the *Guardian* as "the most software-driven warplane ever built," the F-35 Joint Strike Fighter has incurred countless delays and cost overruns totaling billions of dollars. While it has been subject to structural problems and weight issues, the huge amounts of computer code it contains has been a significant source of the warplane's problems. The software was designed to look for problems throughout the plane, but it often failed to work and required lots of time and energy to fix those issues. Cybersecurity is a concern with this highly computerized plane as well, and a lack of testing and protection has hampered development.

THE PEOPLE BEHIND THE WEAPONS

In all branches of the armed forces except the air force, warrant officers serve as technical experts. Though each branch may require slightly different duties, in general warrant officers are in charge of managing and maintaining an array of combat systems, vehicles, and networks. They may train soldiers on technical devices, command and control operations during land combat, and organize the use of equipment during missions.

Army personnel who want to become warrant officers must be selected for warrant officer candidate school, which has similar training to officer candidate school. Typically, warrant officers

Royal Australian Air Force Warrant Officer Adam Tucker operates an optical camera during a search over the south Indian Ocean for the downed Malaysia Airlines flight MH370.

must be members of the military for several years, if not more, before they advance to this position. Army PaYS provides future soldiers and ROTC candidates with a guarantee of a job interview with participating private employers after the completion of their service. Participating companies include CISCO Systems, T-Mobile, and others.

Whether you are interested in becoming a warrant officer or hope to fill another computer-related role in the military, it's a good idea to take classes to familiarize yourself with computer technology. Many of the military's computers use programs developed for uses that do not exist in the civilian world, so you will have to learn their operation in MOS school.

Communication systems operators keep satellite, GPS, and other communications at full capacity. Training includes basic and advanced courses totaling twenty-eight weeks and on-the-job instruction in working with codes and using and maintaining various communications equipment.

This position prepares you for civilian careers as a communications equipment operator at police and fire stations, phone companies, and airports, among others. Candidates are eligible for Army PaYS.

CHAPTER FOUR

THE VIRTUAL AND CYBER WORLDS

Virtual reality (VR) refers to the use of computer models and simulation to create an artificial environment experienced through one's senses.

US Army soldiers in Grafenwoehr, Germany, train using the Dismounted Soldier Training System, the first virtual simulation for

This includes 3D visuals that appear 360 degrees around the user. Sounds enhance the experience, and sometimes the sensation of touch is present if the appropriate gear is used. The intent is to make the user feel as if they are really in the virtual world. VR is experienced by using devices that interact with computers, such as headsets, gloves, goggles, or full body suits. Motion sensors pick up the user's movements and adjust visuals accordingly in real time.

VR has been developed with support from government agencies, most significantly the Department of Defense (DoD). The DoD's primary interest has to do with VR's use as a training tool. By training people in a virtual environment, the military saves money and improves the safety of its troops.

GROUND, AIR, AND SEA TRAINING

For on the ground, the Future Combat System (FCS) is a VR training tool that involves a virtual battle that contains vehicles and weapons. Computer monitors and joystick controllers are attached to a console, allowing trainees to operate simulations of several ground vehicles, such as infantry carriers, mortar vehicles, and reconnaissance vehicles.

The army trains soldiers on how to operate tanks and the Stryker armored vehicle using VR. The VR experience simulates the vehicle's handling in bad terrain or during rain, snow, or other inclement weather conditions. Simulators train soldiers in tactics as well. For instance, modern battlefields can be in cities and towns, which require soldiers to learn how to maneuver around buildings and homes and down streets.

For in the air, VR flight simulators provide visual cues and the sensation of movement to instruct students on how to fly military aircraft, all while the student remains safely on the ground. Students are trained in how to respond to an emergency, fly in battle, and in techniques to link up ground and air forces.

For at sea, the navy uses submarine simulators that provide realistic instrument readings. Some simulators make the module feel as if it is diving or surfacing. The navy also makes use of a virtual bridge. The bridge is an elevated platform on a ship where the captain and officers direct the ship's operations. It includes dozens of computer monitors that allow bridge teams to train as a group through different scenarios. This kind of training builds teamwork and teaches trainees how to handle the ship in the process.

MAKING THE MOVE INTO VR

Careers in the armed forces that make use of VR systems include training instructors and leaders. Changing technology and further developments will likely expand the role of VR in the future. Video game simulations used in the armed forces include "America's Army" and "Guard Force." These games help recruits learn the skills and techniques necessary for a career in the armed forces.

Israeli special combat soldiers make use of Oculus headsets to conduct a VR training exercise simulating underground tunnels leading from Gaza to Israel.

Those looking to enter the VR realm can do so within the armed forces, in a civilian capacity with the armed forces (for instance, the navy recently reported that it employed 267,271 civilian employees), or with a private vendor that supplies the military with equipment. There are a number of steps you can take to prepare yourself to become an attractive candidate for development jobs. Familiarize yourself with VR systems, such as HTC Vive, PlayStation VR, Oculus Rift, Google Daydream (and Google Cardboard), and Samsung Gear VR.

While there are few college majors devoted exclusively to VR or its counterpart, augmented reality (AR), you can steer toward degrees that are more general, such as computer science, mathematics, applied mathematics, engineering, animation, and graphic design.

In an interview with Monster.ca, AR designer Duygo Daniels advises future job seekers to "start learning the basics and demo every AR/VR/AI product you come across. What do you like about these experiences? How would you improve them? Are you interested in how they are made, how they function, or how they look and feel? These questions can help shape what you might want to continue studying."

Networking, or establishing personal connections, is more important in this field than in others because developments in the industry are coming at a fast and furious pace. A good way to keep up is to get to know other enthusiasts at local meet-ups (check for clubs at your school or local Meetup.com groups) or by attending hackathons geared toward VR and AR.

AMONG THE BEST JOBS

In a recent poll, job site Monster.com found that the army, navy, and marines were rated among the best places to work. The armed forces ranked high against private businesses, such as Progressive Insurance, Berkshire Hathaway, and Kaiser Permanente. Reviewers mentioned that the army strives to help soldiers become leaders by providing them with helpful training and mentorship. While working in the army is challenging—among the hardest jobs in the world—it provides a high level of satisfaction. The navy also places a high value on leadership, according to reviewers. One said it was "up to the individual on how far they wanted to go. If you worked hard, you were rewarded appropriately."

CYBERWARFARE

Sophisticated computers that run VR systems and other military devices and vehicles can do amazing things. All indications point to the range of such computing to increase over the coming years. But limitations exist. Training cannot prepare recruits for all circumstances, which experienced soldiers know all too well. Computers can malfunction. Systems can lock. Downloads can take hours instead of minutes.

Wireless communications can work intermittently or not at all. Computer sensors can be confused by camouflage, smoke, and decoys. Bad weather can mess with sensitive equipment.

That's just the beginning, because the rise of sophisticated technology has also spawned a sinister method of warfare: cyberattacks. As the modern world becomes more dependent on computer systems, this form of attack has the potential to cripple expensive networks and reveal sensitive information to enemy

Through the manipulation of code, hackers can conduct cyberwarfare, such as gaining control of computer systems that are vital to the nation's infrastructure.

forces. Cyberwar is different from run-of-the-mill hacking because of its scale and participants. Hackers are usually small-time operators intent on stealing the private information of individuals in order to commit fraud. Cyberwarfare, however, refers to digital attacks made by a nation or country with the intent to commit significant damage.

Cyberwarfare is frightening because so much of modern society and the economy is tied to computer usage. This involves power supplies for entire regions, sanitation, food safety and distribution, and communications (including police and fire departments), not to mention banking and finance systems. These systems can be disabled by electronic bombs (e-bombs) that use high-energy microwave bursts to compromise computer systems and other electronics.

US intelligence agencies have identified countries hostile to US interests and involved in significant cyber threats. They include North Korea, China, Russia, and Iran. Russia in particular has a sophisticated cyber presence and has even been accused of interfering with the 2016 US presidential election.

In August 2017, President Donald Trump gave US Cyber Command, led by Admiral Michael S. Rogers, the status of a Unified Combatant Command, raising it to the level of other major command groups, such as US Central Command and US Pacific Command. This move reflects the increased importance of cyberwarfare efforts. The Department of Defense (DoD) lists three primary missions of the Cyber Mission Force: defend DoD systems, networks, and information; defend the US homeland and US national interests against significant cyberattacks; and provide cyber support to military operations.

CAREERS IN CYBER

Apart from cyberwarfare careers specific to warrant officers, the army has numerous other positions in this realm. One is that of cyber operations specialists, who are responsible for identifying, detecting, and

US Cyber Command consists of components in each military branch, including the Army Cyber Command, the Navy Fleet Cyber Command, Air Force Cyber, and Marine Corps Cyberspace Command.

responding to cyberattacks. Training provided for this position involves certifications useful for civilian as well as military careers and include: CompTIA A+, Network+, and Security+; Certified Ethical Hacker (CEH); Certified Information Systems Security Professional (CISSP); and CISCO Certified Networking Associate (CCNA).

Many government agencies and private security firms hire skilled people in this position, such as the National Security Agency (NSA), Department of Homeland Security (DHS), Federal Bureau of Investigation (FBI), Central Intelligence Agency (CIA), Lockheed Martin Corporation, and Northrop Grumman Corporation. This position guarantees interviews with other private firms through the army's PaYS Program. The air force has a position called cyberspace defense operations with similar duties and requirements.

Those who already have experience as data scientists, web developers, or programmers can join the army's Cyber Direct Commissioning Program to become an officer. As an officer in this field, you will "write algorithms, ciphers, programs and scripts, and conduct research based on your current industry expertise," according to GoArmy.com. This information will be passed along to Cyber Mission Force teams for action. A four-year college degree is required for this program. Check out the US Army Cyber Command website for more information.

Middle school and high school students can participate in the Air Force Association's National Youth Cyber Education Program called CyberPatriot.

The competition involves teams of students who have six hours to find security problems with certain network operating systems while still keeping the system up and running. Teams compete in their region and state, and the winners are sent on an all-expenses-paid trip to Baltimore for the finals competition. If interested, check out the CyberPatriot website. The Air Force Association also holds summer AFA CyberCamps over five-day periods. Camps are located across the country, and fees vary depending on the location.

CHAPTER FIVE

DRONES AND CODE

Aircraft that do not contain crew or passengers are known as unmanned aerial vehicles (UAVs), often referred to as drones. They can be piloted via remote control or on-board guidance systems. They can carry cameras, missiles, or electronic transmitters designed to destroy enemy targets or interfere with their functionality. Because they do not need to support a pilot, drones can be efficient and less expensive than other types of aircraft.

Just like in the private sector, the computer industry changes quickly. Drones are a new technology that the military is keen to use to its fullest extent. Software programming of drones may provide other uses soon, so this is a developing industry. Some drones operate underwater, another avenue of exploration and special programming.

Unmanned aerial vehicles are pilotless aircraft that are operated remotely. Here air force personnel launch a drone on a military mission in the Persian Gulf.

The modern drone came into use extensively during the Vietnam War in the 1960s and 1970s. The most common early drone was the Ryan Firebee, also called the Lightning Bug. The air force flew more than 2,300 Firebees on reconnaissance (recon) missions. Capable of reaching supersonic speeds, they carried a high-resolution camera that allowed them to photograph structures and troops from 1,500 feet (457 m) in the air.

A Lockheed DC-130 plane carried up to four drones and launched them from the sky. After the drone took pictures, it would climb higher into the air and shut off its engines. Parachutes would deploy, and helicopters would attempt to recover the drone in mid-air. If not, they would retrieve it from the ground.

The use of these drones had limitations. Thirty personnel were required for each mission, and each drone could only fly one mission per day. Its navigational capabilities were so inaccurate that they photographed less than half of their planned targets.

MODERN DRONES

The end of the Vietnam War in the mid-1970s meant the air force did not pursue UAV systems until the 1990s. When Iraqi leader Saddam Hussein invaded Kuwait in 1990, the Gulf War ensued. The military buildup was called Operation Desert Shield. Operation Desert Storm took place in early 1991 and consisted of massive US aerial bombardment. Drones had limited use during this operation, with at least one flying at all times. The Israeli-developed Pioneer drone played a significant role in the war effort. It had a wingspan of 17 feet (5.18 m) and length of 14 feet (4.27 m). Its range was around 100 miles (160 km) and flight time about five hours. It carried sensors and cameras that provided battleships with accurate targets that would then be bombed by B-52 or F-15 airplanes.

Drone use has increased in the years since. The United States had about two hundred drones during its 2003 invasion of Iraq. As of July 2013, that number had increased to more than ten thousand. They do everything from dismantling roadside bombs to conducting air strikes. Use of drones is useful for missions that are too dangerous or complex for people. More and more, drones are becoming autonomous, or able to run by making their own decisions as a product of artificial intelligence, rather than via remote control by a human being.

While many drones are used for recon or surveillance, those classified as unmanned combat air vehicles (UCAVs) are used for combat. Called hunter-killers, these machines are armed with bombs, missiles, and sophisticated targeting systems.

Sizes of UAVs vary widely. The pocket-sized Black Hornet Nano is a nanoUAV or microUAV. The 4-pound (1.8 kilogram) RQ-11B Raven resembles a model airplane. Launched by hand, it provides an aerial look to troops in urban areas. The RQ-7 Shadow is about the size of a human being, while the MQ-9 Reaper looks like a small-engine plane. The Reaper and the MQ-1 Predator are hunter-killers. One of the biggest drones is the RQ-4 Global Hawk with a 130-foot (40 m) wingspan.

The Perdix is hand-sized and so fast and high-flying that it requires the use of special high-speed cameras to photograph its flight. Developed by Lincoln Labs at the Massachusetts Institute of Technology (MIT), it is a cheap, expendable device whose transmitters jam enemy radar and confuse their air defenses, especially when they fly in

A service member at the Royal Air Force (RAF) in Waddington, England, displays a Black Hornet drone (*foreground*). In the background is the larger Watchkeeper drone.

swarms of one hundred or more. They also function like miniature spy planes. Their cell phone-quality cameras allow soldiers to hunt down enemies. During combat missions, they launch from F-18 fighter jets.

THE HUMAN COST

Posttraumatic stress disorder (PTSD) is a mental health condition that occurs in some people who experience or witness life-threatening events, such as car accidents, sexual assaults, natural disasters, or combat. Symptoms include flashbacks that make people feel as though they are experiencing the event again, feeling keyed up, angry outbursts, bad memories, nightmares, guilt, shame, and loss of interest in activities that were previously enjoyable. It is a significant problem, with the National Institutes of Health (NIH) estimating that 11 percent of veterans of the war in Afghanistan and 20 percent of veterans of the Iraq War experience it.

PTSD and other mental health problems can affect drone operators due to the nature of drone attacks. Drone deaths of enemy combatants—and civilians—can number in the thousands without the drone operator putting himself or herself in danger. Although drone strikes may seem similar to shots fired in video games, it's important to realize they have real consequences for US forces as well as the enemy.

An ocean-going drone called the Sea Hunter tracks submarines autonomously. It costs a fraction of the price of a warship and can travel about 10,000 nautical miles (16,090 km) on one (very large) tank of gas.

POSITIONS AND PREPARATION

The air force has a dedicated UAV operator job classification, and the army offers a similar position called unmanned aircraft systems operator.

Operators must assess intelligence gathered from the drone and make life-or-death decisions on the

Unmanned aerial vehicles come in all sizes. Some are even small enough to launch by hand, as is this Small Unmanned Aircraft System (SUAS) by Marine Corps Corporal Jonathan Kim.

fly in fast-moving conditions. The air force requires that operators have a college degree and become commissioned officers to operate drones, but the other services do not.

The army refers to its drone operators as intelligence specialists and requires twenty-three weeks of advanced training and on-the-job instruction in addition to ten weeks of basic combat training before operators are qualified. The drone operator position is affiliated with the PaYS Program that, upon release from military service, guarantees interviews with military-friendly employers such as Lockheed Martin and Raytheon. Lockheed Martin's Advanced Development Programs ("Skunk Works") specializes in designing and producing advanced aircraft, including drones.

Students interested in this career path should steer toward classes in science (especially physics), computer science, design, math, and engineering. Training programs are popping up at colleges and universities and at dedicated schools like the Unmanned Vehicle University (UVU) in Phoenix, Arizona. Otherwise, you can train on-the-job in the military.

Prior to enlistment or entering college, the best way to learn about drones and gather helpful experience is to experiment with them at home, school, or in a local club. Some drones are simple, inexpensive, and easily learned, such as quadcopters. Others are much more expensive and complicated. Familiarize yourself with the FAA's Small Unmanned Aircraft Rule, which gives guidelines for drones like the weight limits (less than 55 pounds [25 kg]), hours of operation (daylight), maximum speed and altitude, and restrictions about where drones can be legally flown. Advanced usage may require a drone pilot certification.

The future of drone operations careers looks bright as technology advances and new and innovative uses are attempted. One of those innovations occurred in July 2015, when the British Navy ship HMS *Mersey* assembled an inexpensive drone that had been created using a 3D printer and launched it off its gun deck. It handled ocean winds and rolling swell, and it opened the door for creating and using disposable plastic drones for a number of military missions.

CHAPTER SIX

MILITARY ROBOTICS

Robots used to be a mainstay of science fiction books, TV shows, and movies. *Lost in Space* had a robot crew member that warned of danger in many episodes. *Star Wars* had R2D2 and C3PO in the original film, and *Star Wars: The Last Jedi* had BB-8. Some writers and filmmakers portray robots as cute and helpful, while others have them taking over the world and destroying humanity.

Robotics is big business these days. The industry is predicted to total $67 billion by 2025 as technology gets cheaper and more efficient. Robots in use in private industry, government and law enforcement, and the military come in many shapes and sizes.

The simple definition of a robot is a machine that carries out a complex set of actions automatically and is programmed by a computer. It can operate in the air or on the ground. Robots consist of moving parts that allow them to interact with their surroundings and perform certain tasks, such as gripping a screwdriver or lifting a rock. They have multiple sensors designed to keep the unit from hitting obstacles, such as walls, rocks, or people. They also come equipped with devices such as cameras and microphones. Robots can be programmed to initiate certain actions or gather data to be analyzed later. They can be controlled remotely by a human operator.

THE FUNCTIONS OF ROBOTS

In the military, robots serve different functions. They can carry heavy equipment, handle dangerous materials, spy on the enemy, and assist in medical procedures. The government is testing a four-legged "mule" robot called the Legged Squad Support System that can carry supplies to soldiers across rocky landscapes.

MARCbot is a small robot used to inspect suspicious objects like bombs. TALON robots are small as well, weighing less than 100 pounds (45 kg). They are durable enough to survive falling off bridges into rivers. They can be equipped with sensors to locate mines, IEDs (improvised explosive devices), and dangerous chemicals. Gripper claws allow these robots to move explosives and other dangerous objects away from people.

TALON robots were modified and adapted to create the Special Weapons Observation Reconnaissance Detection System (SWORDS). These robots carry grenade launchers, flamethrowers, automatic rifles,

Marine Corps Warfighting Lab personnel conduct a training exercise with the experimental Legged Squad Support System (LS3) around the Kahuku Training Area in Hawaii.

and machine guns. Other robots are designed for combat, such as Mesa Associates' Tactical Integrated Light-Force Deployment Assembly (MATILDA) and Modular Advanced Armed Robotic System (MAARS).

Robots can assist soldiers fighting in urban areas. The MARCbot and PackBot (a small robot about 40 pounds [18 kg] operating on treads) can be sent ahead to disarm traps and identify enemy fighters. They can look around corners and up into windows.

The navy revealed a firefighting robot prototype called Shipboard Autonomous Firefighting Robot, or

SAFFiR (pronounced "safer"). It was developed by researchers at Virginia Tech to resemble a human by having two legs. It can move around a ship, open doors, handle fire hoses, and use sensors to see through smoke. Though it can act on its own, it takes instructions from remote operators.

Office of Naval Research program manager Thomas McKenna notes, "We're working toward human-robot teams. It's what we call the hybrid force: humans and robots working together."

INTERNET OF THINGS

One of the most popular ideas these days is the Internet of Things (IoT). What does that mean? Devices that have the ability to connect to the internet fall under this category—but only those that are usually "dumb." Basically, it's anything that can be connected and/or controlled via the internet, such as a light bulb that can be switched on or off using a smartphone app. It could be a driverless car, or a smart thermostat that adjusts temperature in your office depending on a sensor's input. Or maybe it is an alarm clock that goes off at 7:00 am and automatically starts your coffee maker. Some of the most important devices in the IoT are appliances, vehicles, and wearable gadgets.

However, US intelligence has warned that all this internet connection may be a bad thing. Cameras, cookers, thermostats, and other devices connected to the internet might be used to spy on people in their homes. That's not as outrageous as it sounds when you consider that devices such as Amazon's Echo listen to the words you speak and respond with information like the weather forecast, a phone number, traffic updates, and more.

The army has issued helmets with built-in sensors to help diagnose brain injuries. Individual munitions now have internet addresses. Everything from bombs to nuclear weapons, communications, satellites, vehicles, armor, lasers, and navigational systems depends on computers. And all these systems need to be protected from digital tampering.

PREPARING FOR A CAREER IN MILITARY ROBOTICS

Whether you are in middle school or high school, there are plenty of opportunities for you to learn about robotics if you look for them. Depending on your location, you may be able to attend a summer tech camp such as those put on by iD Tech. Camps are located in twenty-nine states and internationally in Hong Kong, Singapore, and the United Kingdom. The Robocoder camp serves ages seven through nine and makes use of LEGO MINDSTORMS EV3. Participants work in teams to create robots.

An employee with a London, England, toy shop operates a LEGO Mindstorms EV3 robot from a tablet computer.

Wearable Tech is designed for girls aged ten through fifteen making use of LilyPad Arduino. The Robotics Engineering and Coding Lab with VEX Robotics Design System is geared toward those aged thirteen through seventeen. Participants work in teams to adapt robots to challenges.

First LEGO League brings young people together with adult coaches to form teams that tackle real-world problems, such as recycling, energy, and food safety. In addition, teams must design, construct, and program a robot that can compete on a tabletop using

LEGO MINDSTORMS. More than 255,000 participants in eighty-eight countries have built 32,000 robots. Check out the website for more information.

The YMCA offers summer tech camps at many of its 2,700 locations in the United States alone. You can find other camps and competitions through your local library or school.

While an in-person computer camp or event may be fun and helpful, these are not an option for everyone due to location, cost, or other factors. There are a number of good online options that are free of cost. NASA runs the Robotics Alliance Project, whose mission is "to create a human, technical, and programmatic resource of robotics capabilities to enable the implementation of future robotic space exploration missions." Check out its website at robotics.nasa.gov for a wealth of information on events, projects, challenges, and more.

RobotBASIC is a free robotics program created by two retired college professors. It teaches students to program by simulating a robot with sensors, wireless controls, animated simulations, and video games. The goal is to motivate students to learn and design contests for robot clubs.

JOBS IN ROBOTICS

The US Army Research Laboratory runs the Robotics Collaborative Technology Alliance to develop robotic tech for future use by soldiers. It has a number of affiliated institutions, such as Florida State University,

Carnegie Mellon University, and MIT. Military labs have outreach programs that employ student interns of various grades and levels in science, technology, engineering, and mathematics (STEM) fields.

The army offers a career as an engineer officer with a wide range of duties, including training soldiers and researching alternative technology. The US Army Corps of Engineers includes 30,000 civilian and 750 military engineers. This position is eligible for the PaYS Program as well. The navy employs robotics technicians under the broader category of electronics technicians. After nine weeks of training in basic electronics, the candidate attends forty-two weeks of advanced training. Coursework or interest in arithmetic, computer science, and electronics before enlistment is helpful in qualifying for this position.

ROBOTICS RESEARCH

Much of the high-tech, computer-driven devices used by the military have been developed due to research by DARPA (Defense Advanced Research Project Agency). Always on the cutting edge, one example of their skills is their invention—in just sixty-six days—of an electronic sniper-detection device called Boomerang. It consisted of microphones mounted to a tall aluminum pole that sits atop armored vehicles. The microphones listen for the sound of a sniper's rifle–specifically the shockwaves of a speeding bullet–and program this info into a computer. The computer

The CHIMP (Carnegie Mellon University Highly Intelligent Mobile Platform) robot uses a handheld drill in the Defense Advanced Research Projects Agency (DARPA) Robotics Challenge.

analyzes the data in less than a second and pinpoints where the shot came from. This allows soldiers to respond to the threat immediately and accurately.

The US Naval Research Lab in Washington, D.C., is responsible for many advanced technologies in the military today, especially with communications and undersea warfare, space systems, tactics, and microelectronics.

MEDICINE AND COMPUTERS

Emerging technology targeted at efficiently and effectively attending to battlefield injuries is an important area of research. DARPA research under development involves chips implanted into a soldier's brain. These will download signals from certain brain activities. If the individual's brain is injured, those signals may be able to be uploaded into the brain to restore functionality.

The army is developing robots for medical uses, focusing on removing wounded soldiers from the battlefield and providing them with medical attention as soon as possible, improving their chances of survival. Unmanned ambulances could accomplish this without putting human medics' lives at risk. Robots could also deliver medical supplies to soldiers in enemy territory.

THE FUTURE

Computer science is likely to play an ever more important role as the twenty-first century unfolds. This includes the increased use of algorithms, robots, and artificial intelligence. FAWs, or fully autonomous weapons, are robots that will reduce the need for human soldiers on the battlefield. They

🔋 65% ⬛ 4:38 PM

CATALOG ITEMS

First aid kit	?	-	0	+
Tourniquet	?	-	0	+
Canteen	?	-	1	+
Magazine	?	-	0	+
Grenade	?	-	0	+
Shotgun shell	?	-	0	+
40mm NATO round	?	-	0	+

1 ▾   SETUP DELIVERY

Callsign: BLACKBIRD
18S TH 85366 65882
339 ft MSL
0 MPH   +/- 5m

BACK   Show View... ▾

72 m

US Marine personnel fly Hive drones at a demonstration on the Marine base at Quantico, Virginia. The drones are designed to streamline resupply to combat fighters.

will contain computers that will be programmed to carry out missions. They are in development now and nowhere near capable of taking the place of human soldiers—yet.

In 2014, the Army Research Laboratory asked a group of experts to predict what war would look like in 2050. They said the following:

- Augmented/enhanced humans (including genetic modifications and body armor).
- Robot swarms both independently operated and under the control of humans. Some may be the size of insects. Others may operate underwater.

- Automated decision making and processes using AI.
- Predictions and simulations of enemy behaviors.
- Threats to information, such as hacking, misinformation, and dense electronic warfare.
- Targeting of individuals based on their unique electronic and behavioral signatures—a real possibility since projects are underway to identify people at a distance from the shape of their ears and gaits, fingerprint scanners that work at a distance, chemical markers in sweat, and specifics of one's heartbeat, among other things.
- Sensors everywhere will collect vast amounts of information—such as face and eye scans—and make use of that info. These come from drones, satellites, computer spying, and communications intercepts, among other things.

The future holds vast opportunities for computer-related careers in the military. You can be a part of them with preparation, determination, and the proper training.

algorithm A set of steps to complete a computer process.

augmented reality The overlay of real-time computer-generated information on the physical environment.

bit A unit of computer information that is expressed as a 0 or 1.

casualties Those in the military who can no longer fight due to death, injury, capture, or other condition.

circuit board Many electrical circuits attached to a board.

civilian A person not on active duty for the armed forces.

command A written instruction that directs the computer to take a certain action.

debug To fix problems in the functioning of computer programs.

enlisted A person enrolled in the armed forces.

GI Bill A law that provides benefits such as educational assistance for former members of the military.

hackathon A competition that involves manipulation of computer software for a purpose other than which it was intended.

hardware The physical components of a computer.

infrastructure The basic structures, such as roads and bridges, that allow a country or area to function properly.

logistical Having to do with organization and planning.

military occupational specialty (MOS) The job for which a military member is trained.

operating system Software that allows users to access a computer's basic functions.

private sector Part of the national economy that is not controlled by the government.

Reserve Officers' Training Corps (ROTC) A college-based officer training program.

software Programs that direct a computer to perform certain functions.

vendor A company or person offering something for sale.

virtual reality A simulated 3D environment generated by computers that allows a person to interact with it physically by the use of special electronic equipment such as a visor.

FOR MORE INFORMATION

CIPS National Office
1375 Southdown Road
Unit 16 - Suite 802
Mississauga, ON L5J 2Z1
Canada
(877) ASK-CIPS (275-2477)
Website: http://www.cips.ca
Facebook: CIPS.ca
Offers networking opportunities, certification of
    IT professionals (I.S.P. and ITCP designations),
    accreditation of IT university and college programs,
    and an IT job board.

Defense Advanced Research Projects Agency (DARPA)
675 North Randolph Street
Arlington, VA 22203-2114
(703) 526-6630
Website: https://www.darpa.mil
Facebook and Twitter: @darpa
An official Department of Defense website
    that highlights DARPA's mission of strategic
    technological excellence for the US military.
    Extensive information on research, news, events,
    and career opportunities is provided.

Military.com
55 Second Street, Suite 300
San Francisco, CA 94105
customersupport@military.com
Website: https://www.military.com

Facebook, Twitter, and Instagram: @militarydotcom
The largest online organization for the military and
veterans at ten million members. Its mission
is to connect the military community to all the
advantages connected with service to America.

US Department of Defense (DoD)
Public Communications
1400 Defense Pentagon
Washington, DC 20301-1400
(703) 571-3343
Website: https://www.defense.gov
Facebook, Twitter, and Instagram: @deptofdefense
The DoD's mission is to "provide a lethal Joint Force
to defend the security of our country and sustain
American influence abroad." It is the central point
of contact for the Joint Chiefs of Staff, the army,
navy, marines, air force, and Coast Guard, as well
as numerous unified combatant commands.

FOR FURTHER READING

Bedell, Jane (J. M.). *So, You Want to Be a Coder?* New York, NY: Simon & Schuster, 2016.

Burgan, Michael. *Weapons Technology.* New York, NY: Scholastic, Inc., 2017.

Faust, Daniel R. *Military Drones.* New York, NY: Rosen Publishing Group, Inc., 2016.

Johnson, Cynthia, and Chris Womack. *ASVAB Demystified.* New York, NY: McGraw-Hill, 2013.

Kassnoff, David. *What Degree Do I Need to Pursue a Career in Information Technology & Information Systems?* New York, NY: Rosen Publishing, 2015.

LearningExpress. *Officer Candidate Tests: Complete Preparation for the ASVAB, AFOQT, and ASTB.* 2nd Edition. New York, NY: LearningExpress, 2017.

Mara, Wil. *Software Development.* New York, NY: Scholastic, Inc., 2016.

McKinney, Devon. *A Day at Work with a Software Developer.* New York, NY: PowerKids Press, Rosen Publishing, 2016.

Perritano, John. *War and the Military.* Broomhill, PA: Mason Crest, 2017.

Saujani, Reshma. *Girls Who Code: Learn to Code and Change the World.* New York, NY: Viking, Penguin Young Readers Group, 2017.

Air Force Association's Cyberpatriot. "Program Overview." Retrieved March 2, 2018. http://www.uscyberpatriot.org/Documents/Fact%20 Sheets/10.03%20ProgramOverview.pdf.

Air Force Association's Cyberpatriot. "Want to Attend an AFA Cybercamp?" Retrieved March 2, 2018. http://uscyberpatriot.org/special-initiatives /afa-cybercamp-programwant-to-attend -an-afa-cybercamp.

Bedell, Jane (J.M.). *So, You Want to Be a Coder?* New York, NY: Simon & Schuster, 2016.

Brown, Sean Mclain. "Army, Navy, Marine Corps Rated Among Best Places to Work." Military.com. Retrieved March 1, 2018. https://www.military .com/join-armed-forces/army-marine-corps-navy -rated-best-places-to-work.html.

Bureau of Labor Statistics, US Department of Labor. *Occupational Outlook Handbook*, Military Careers. Retrieved January 18, 2018. https://www.bls.gov /ooh/military/military-careers.htm.

Digital History. "Truman's Diary on the Atomic Bomb." Retrieved April 24, 2018. http://www.digitalhistory .uh.edu/disp_textbook.cfm?smtID=3&psid=1186.

Economist. "Up in the Air." March 29, 2014. https:// www.economist.com/news/specialreport /21599524-drones-will-change -warand-more-up-air.

Eldor, Karin. "Are You Considering a Career In Augmented/Virtual Reality or Artificial Intelligence?" Monster.ca. Retrieved March 2, 2018. https://

www.monster.ca/career-advice/article/consider-a-career-in-artificial-intelligence.

First LEGO League. "What Is First LEGO League?" Retrieved March 4, 2018. http://www.firstlegoleague.org/about-fll.

Frontline. "Weapons: Drones." PBS. Retrieved March 3, 2018. https://www.pbs.org/wgbh/pages/frontline/gulf/weapons/drones.html.

Garamone, Jim, and Lisa Ferdinando. "DoD Initiates Process to Elevate U.S. Cyber Command to Unified Combatant Command." US Department of Defense, August 18, 2017. https://www.defense.gov/News/Article/Article/1283326/dod-initiates-process-to-elevate-us-cyber-command-to-unified-combatant-command.

Gibbs, Samuel. "Radar Glitch Requires F-35 Fighter Jet Pilots to Turn It Off and On Again." *Guardian*, March 8, 2016. https://www.theguardian.com/technology/2016/mar/08/radar-glitch-requires-f-35-fighter-jet-pilots-to-turn-it-off-and-on-again.

Grabianowski, Ed. "How Military Robots Work." HowStuffWorks.com, January 19, 2005. https://science.howstuffworks.com/military-robot.htm.

Latiff, Robert H. *Future War: Preparing for the New Global Battlefield*. New York, NY: Penguin Random House, 2017.

Luckwaldt, Adam. "Air Force Unmanned Aerial Vehicle Operator Career." The Balance, April 16, 2017. https://www.thebalance.com/career-profile-air-force-unmanned-aerial-vehicle-operator-2356488.

Mahnken, Thomas G. *Technology and the American Way of War Since 1945*. New York, NY: Columbia University Press, 2008.

Marks, Paul. "British Navy Warship Tests a 3-D-Printed Drone at Sea." *MIT Technology Review*, July 22, 2015. https://www.technologyreview .com/s/539586british-navy-warship-tests-a-3 -d-printed-drone-at-sea.

Martin, David. "New Generation of Drones Set to Revolutionize Warfare." *CBS News*, August 20, 2017. https://www.cbsnews.com/news/60- minutes-autonomous-drones-set-to -revolutionize-military-technology-2.

Military.com. "Comparing Military Pay and Benefits to Civilian Jobs." Retrieved February 21, 2018. https://www.military.com/join-armed-forces /military-vs-civilian-benefits-overview.html.

Militaryspot.com. "Understanding the Five Branches of the Military." Retrieved February 21, 2018. http://www.militaryspot.com/enlist/understanding -the-five-branches-of-the-military.

NASA. "Robotics Alliance Project Mission." Retrieved March 4, 2018. https://robotics.nasa.gov /mission.php.

NIH MedlinePlus. "PTSD: A Growing Epidemic." Winter 2009. https://medlineplus.gov/magazine/issues /winter09/articles/winter09pg10-14.html.

Onrec.co. "Immersive Virtual Reality Recruitment as the Future of Job Market." June 29, 2017. http:// www.onrec.com/news/news-archive/immersive -virtual-reality-recruitment-as-the-future-of-job-market.

Pilkington, Ed. "Life as a Drone Operator: 'Ever Step on Ants and Never Give It Another Thought?'" *Guardian*, November 19, 2015. https://www .theguardian.com/world/2015/nov/18/life-as -a-drone -pilot-creech-air-force-base-nevada.

PTSD: National Center for PTSD. "What Is PTSD?" US Department of Veterans Affairs. Retrieved March 3, 2018. https://www.ptsd.va.gov/public/PTSD -overview/basics/what-is-ptsd.asp.

Ranger, Steve. "Cyberwar: A Guide to the Frightening Future of Online Conflict." ZDNet, August 29, 2017. http://www.zdnet.com/article/cyberwar-a-guide-to -the-frightening-future-of-online-conflict.

Ranger, Steve. "What is the IoT? Everything You Need to Know about the Internet of Things Right Now." ZDNet, January 19, 2018. http://www.zdnet.com /article/what-is-the-internet-of-things-everything-you -need-to-know-about-the-iot-right-now.

Sandia National Laboratories. "Sandia's Self-guided Bullet Prototype Can Hit Target a Mile Away." January 30, 2012. https://share-ng.sandia. gov/news/resources/news_releases/bullet /#Wo8Tq6inGM8.

Sass, Erik. "12 Technological Advancements of World War I." Mental Floss, April 30, 2017. http:// mentalfloss.com/article/31882/12-technological -advancements-world-war-i.

Saujani, Reshma. *Girls Who Code: Learn to Code and Change the World.* New York, NY: Viking, Penguin Young Readers Group, 2017.

Sisk, Richard. "Cyber Command to Become Unified Combatant Command." Military.com. Retrieved March 2, 2018. https://www.military.com/daily -news/2017/08/18/cyber-command-become -unified-combatant-command.html.

Statista. "Inventory of Unmanned Aerial Systems (UAS) Commonly Known as Drones of the US Military as of July 1, 2013." July 1, 2013. https://

www.statista.com/statistics/428793/us-military
-inventory-of-unmanned-aerial-systems-or-drones.

Stix, Gary. "The Stirrup." *Scientific American*,
September 1, 2009. https://www
.scientificamerican.com/article/the-stirrup.

Strickland, Jonathan. "How Virtual Reality Military
Applications Work." HowStuffWorks.com, August
27, 2007. https://science.howstuffworks.com
/virtual-military.htm.

Terdiman, Daniel. "VR Will Be a $38 Billion Industry by
2026: Report." *Fast Company*, November 2, 2016.
https://www.fastcompany.com/3065227
/vr-will-be-a-38-billion-industry-by-2026-report.

Today's Military. "Types of Military Service." Retrieved
February 21, 2018. https://todaysmilitary.com
/joining/types-of-military-service.

US Army. "Careers & Jobs: Warrant Officer Corps
(09W)." Retrieved February 22, 2018. https://www
.goarmy.com/careers-and-jobs/browse-career
-and-job-categories/computers-and-technology
/warrant-officer-corps.html.

US Army. "Cyber Direct Commissioning Program."
Retrieved March 2, 2018. https://www.goarmy
.com/army-cyber/cyber-direct-commissioning
-program.html.

US Army. "Cyber Operations Specialist (17C)."
Retrieved March 2, 2018. https://www.goarmy
.com/careers-and-jobs/browse-career-and-job
-categories/computers-and-technology/cyber
-operations-specialist.html.

US Army. "Join the Partnership." Retrieved February 22,
2018. https://www.armypays.com/INDEX2.html.

US Army. "Learn How to Join." Retrieved February 21, 2018. https://www.goarmy.com/learn /understanding-the-asvab.html.

US Army. "Unmanned Aircraft Systems Operator (15W)." Retrieved March 3, 2018. https://www .goarmy.com/careers-and-jobs/browse-career -and-job-categories/transportation-and-aviation /unmanned-aerial-vehicle-operator.html.

US Army Acquisition Support Center. "Common Remotely Operated Weapon Station (CROWS)." Retrieved February 22, 2018. http://asc.army.mil /web/portfolio-item/common-remotely-operated -weapon-station-crows.

US Army Research Laboratory. "Robotics." Retrieved March 4, 2018. https://www.arl.army.mil/www /default.cfm?page=392.

US Army Research Laboratory. "Student Interns for Military Laboratories GEMS, SEAP, and CQL." Retrieved March 4, 2018. https://www.arl.army .mil/www/default.cfm?page=1519.

US Department of Defense. "The Department of Defense Cyber Strategy." Retrieved March 2, 2018. https://www.defense.gov/News/Special-Reports /0415_Cyber-Strategy.

US Department of Veterans Affairs. "America's Wars." Retrieved April 24, 2018. https://www.va.gov/opa /publications/factsheets/fs_americas_wars.pdf.

US History. "51f. The Manhattan Project." Retrieved April 24, 2018. http://www.ushistory.org/us /51f.asp.

US Navy. "Electronics: Training & Advancement." Retrieved March 4, 2018. https://www.navy.com

/careers/engineering-applied-science/electronics
.html#ft-training-&-advancement.

US Navy. "Status of the Navy." December 31, 2017.
http://www.navy.mil/navydata/nav_legacy
.asp?id=146.

US Navy Fact File. *TOMAHAWK* CRUISE MISSILE."
Retrieved February 22, 2018. http://www.navy.mil
/navydata/fact_display
.asp?cid=2200&tid=1300&ct=2.

Ward, B.S., Lt. Colonel, Retired, USAF. Phone Interview.
January 13, 2017.

White, Tammy. "Making Sailors 'SAFFiR'—Navy Unveils
Firefighting Robot Prototype at Naval Tech EXPO."
US Navy, February 4, 2015. http://www.navy.mil
/submit/display.asp?story_id=85459.

ABOUT THE AUTHOR

Xina M. Uhl has written numerous educational books for young people. She has tackled subjects including history, biographies, technology, and health concerns. Growing up, she listened to tales of her father's army deployments in Europe and resolved to travel to those places one day. Her blog details her travels, publications, history tidbits, and the occasional cat picture.

PHOTO CREDITS

Cover Gorondenkoff/Shutterstock.com; back cover, pp. 4–5 (background) and interior pages nadla/E+/Getty Images; p. 5 US Navy photo by Mass Communication Specialist Second Class Brent Pyfrom; pp. 8, 16, 25, 33, 44, 53 Andrey_Popov/Shutterstock.com; p. 9 Sovfoto/Universal Images Group/Getty Images; p. 13 Ivan Cholakov/Shutterstock.com; p. 17 US Army photo by Sgt. Roland Hale, 1st Inf. Div. Public Affairs; p. 21 US Navy photo by Mass Communication Specialist 1st Class Alexandra Seeley; p. 27 Riccardo Niccoli/Stocktrek Images/Getty Images; p. 29 US Navy photo by John F. William; p. 31 Xinhua/Alamy Stock Photo; p. 33 US Army Photo by Visual Information Specialist Markus Rauchenberger; p. 36 Bloomberg/Getty Images; p. 39 BEST-BACKGROUNDS/Shutterstock.com; p. 41 US Army; p. 45 John Moore/Getty Images; p. 48 Nigel Roddis/Getty Images;p. 50 US Marine Corps photo by Lance Cpl. Dalton Swanbeck;p. 55 Stocktrek Images, Inc./Alamy Stock Photo; p. 58 Oli Scarff/Getty Images; p. 61 Chip Somodevilla/Getty Images;p. 63 Frances Seybold /Marine Corps Base Quantico/DVIDS; interior design graphic (abstract circuit) Titima Ongkantong/Shutterstock.com.

Design: Michael Moy; Layout: Nicole Russo-Duca; Photo Researcher: Karen Huang